# Patterns of
# PRAISE

## Major Religious Art Works
### SR. HELENA STEFFENS-MEIER
### School Sisters of Saint Francis
### Artist-in-Residence, Alverno College

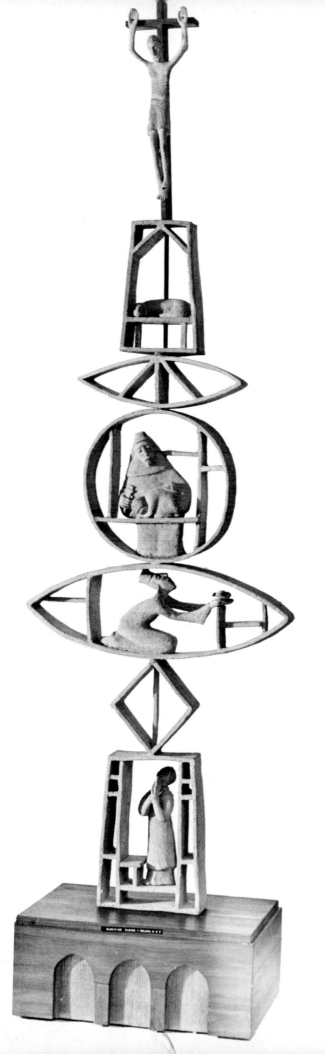

# AN APPRECIATION

The work of Sister Helena Steffens-meier expresses tenderness toward humankind, strength and joy in facing the demands of creative work, boundless spontaneity, and dignity. An unflagging feeling for formal design contributes to Helena's power to release emotional effects of such rich dimensions in a variety of media.

Serenity is the dominant mood of her work. It is a serenity that tells of the kind of universal wisdom often expressed in archaic art. It is a serenity strengthened by struggle—the marks of which are especially visible in her stone and wood sculptures. These sculptures embody the struggle, involving her whole psyche and expressed through her strong hands, to aesthetically reveal her unreserved faith in God's goodness.

Sister Helena believes that "art is the most intimate expression of one's most intimate life." Her works reveal the charismatic forms of both her art and her life.

Her career as an artist is characterized by the interaction of design and spontaneity in her life. Out of the texture of her professional life as a religious, art gradually emerged as a single, consuming focus.

In 1917 she left her hometown of St. Paul, Iowa to join the School Sisters of St. Francis in Milwaukee and then taught in elementary schools in Iowa and Nebraska. Later she taught English, religion, algebra, and art in Aurora and Chicago high schools. During these teaching years she also obtained a Master of Arts degree at DePaul University and further art training at the Chicago Art Institute and the Catholic University of America.

While in Chicago she became a companion to a sister who was studying sculpture with the famous Viennese sculptor, Emil Zettler. Zettler gave Helena some clay, too, and she promptly modeled a figure which drew his praise. He pointed out the foot, although anatomically wrong, was aesthetically right and that it showed her innate sense of design.

On a second occasion when she had offered to decorate rooms in the convent for a festal day and did it so effectively, the head of the convent's art department declared her an artist with much potential.

Patience and obedience in carrying out her former tasks ultimately brought Helena to her heart's desire—to create art and to teach it. Years of working with young people no doubt contributed to her ability to approach both subjects and media with freshness. She was able to enter the world of the young with sensitivity, lightheartedness, and compassion—qualities that she now combines with the objective understanding of the wise.

In 1950 she was assigned to Alverno College, where she taught art and ultimately became head of the art department. Through the inspiration and disciplined direction she gave to a multitude of students who became professional artists and teachers, she and her staff developed the department to one of size and stature. In 1971 she was named Professor Emeritus and Artist-in-Residence. Many of her art works are housed at Alverno.

Although she is tiny in stature and seemingly fragile in physique, Helena's strength and determination is evidenced in monumental sculptures chiseled from stone and wood. In whatever forms stone and wood come to her, she intuitively sees a subject and senses how best she can disclose it with her chisel.

She undertakes the discipline of a carver who must, with unerring skill, take away whatever stands in the way of the form waiting within; the form toward which her creative spirit surges. To her students, she emphasized that "subtractive sculpture lends itself to a more formal approach and resists facile surface handling."

The Tennessee marble "Pieta," reproduced on the cover page is measured in inches, yet it is no less monumental in its form and message than "Sacrifice," the seven foot stoneware sculpture shown on the title page. All the ramifications of sacrificial suffering are intrinsic in both. Material and concept have become entities in these, as in all her sculpture. "Fatherhood," created after she worked with the poor of Guatemala in 1969, tells in limestone of the eternal unity between parent and child. The idea is powerfully projected while the stoniness of the medium remains intact.

CIBORIUM
Silver, moss agates

CHALICE
Silver. ebony

ROSARY
Silver, ebony

PECTORAL CROSS
Ebony, ivory, bloodstone

ST. CHRISTOPHER
Silver, ebony

Helena has said that materials influence her very much. "Wood asks for more warmth in handling because it is an organic, living thing, and stone demands more austere and elemental treatment." Thus, in "Ruth and Naomi," another objectified expression of charismatic togetherness, the wood from which the sculpture was chiseled remains plainly the stuff of the walnut trunk in which the figures waited while the tree aspired toward the sky.

Sojourns in Guatemala and Costa Rica intensified Helena's identification with primitivism and gave new freedom to her use of color, which is particularly expressed in her recent stitchery and sculpture, such as "Trinity in Communion." In this unearthly conception, the Divine Spirit is a tongue of roughly-chipped, red-gold slab glass blazing between the Father and Son who are conceived as soaring massive wings of dark cherry wood.

Helena's stitchery, often large and rich with images and symbolism, are most often emblems of celebration. "Prodigal Son," is especially such a manifestation. In it she expresses joy—like that of her hanging which quotes Socrates, "take joy home and make a place in your heart for her."

Helena's status in her religious community as well as in the community-at-large, among non-Catholics as well as members of the Church, has grown with the years. Now, at 76, she remains intent on finding "newness" in creating art. Always open herself, she finds the renewal of the church and its openness a source for self-growth. Recently, she expressed her intuitions about these developments in a praying alabaster figure whose hands are held up on either side of the face with the palms faced outward, signifying unreserved generous trust. It is entitled, "Lord, Here I Am."

The titles of the works listed in this book, the variety of media, the range of sizes—all indicate the challenging course Helena has followed with burning faith. She has dealt with many themes, but the content of her work—the message she has for viewers—has remained constant. It is expressed in the title of this volume, "Patterns of Praise."

—Margaret Fish Rahill
Curator, Charles Allis Library, Milwaukee

ST. HELENA
Walnut
29"

DETAIL

ST. FRANCIS
Mahogany
60"

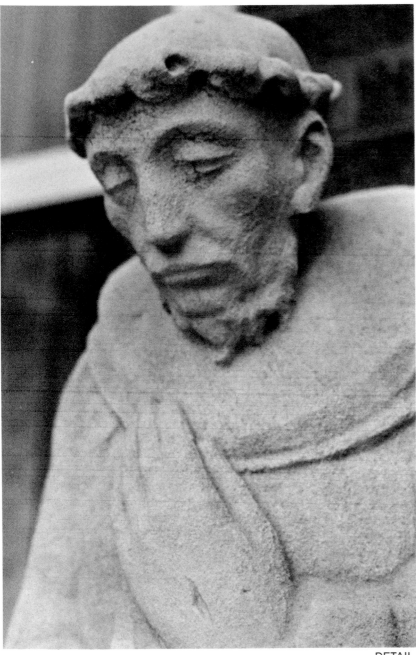

DETAIL

ST. FRANCIS
Caenstone
36"

SEDES SAPIENTIAE
Stoneware
70"

CHRIST AMENING
THE FATHER
Aluminum
72"

CRUCIFIX "IT IS FINISHED"
Ceramic
97½"

DETAIL

DAVID AND JONATHAN
Blue Connecticut marble
21"

HEAD OF ST. FRANCIS
Stone boulder
19"

ANGEL OF JUDGMENT
Rosestone
24"

10

VIRGIN MARTYR
Limestone
10½"

12

TOWER OF IVORY
Applewood
65"

SAINT CLARE
Granite
36"

CRECHE
Stoneware
31"

13

THE NEW PASSOVER
Stoneware
27"

QUEEN MOTHER
Walnut
25″

CRUCIFIX
Birch
54″

15

MADONNA AND CHILD
Oak
25"

SAINT HELENA
Walnut
24"

NINE CHOIRS OF ANGELS    Oil    33¼" x 124"

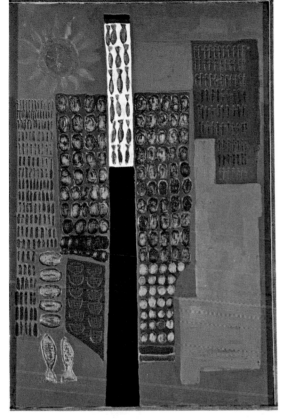

MIRACLE OF LOAVES AND FISHES   Oil   40½" x 27"

STIGMATA OF
ST. FRANCIS
Oil
57" x 27½"

SCENES FROM THE LIFE OF CHRIST
Acrylic on wood    31" x 25"

RAISING OF LAZARUS
Oil
27½" x 30½"

GOSPEL STORY
Stitching and applique
92" x 30"

PAROUSIA
Oil
22½" x 43"

DETAIL

DESCENT OF THE HOLY SPIRIT
Oil    46" x 38½"

"TAKE JOY HOME"   Stitching and applique    99" x 50"

"IN MY FATHER'S HOUSE THERE ARE
MANY MANSIONS"   Oil   25¾" x 32"

"I AM THE RESURRECTION AND THE LIFE"
Oil
43" x 22"

19

"I HAVE FOUND THE SHEEP THAT WAS LOST"
Stitching
52½" x 49"

DEATH OF ST. FRANCIS
Watercolor
23¼" x 36½"

DETAIL

ALLELUIA
Stitching and applique
86" x 36"

CRECHE
Polychromed wood
25"

LAST SUPPER
Cloissone
8"

PRODIGAL SON
Stitching and applique
48" x 81"

MOTHER AND CHILD
Stitching
47½ x 40"

23

"AND THE BIRDS MADE
THEIR NESTS
IN ITS BRANCHES"
Stitching
67" x 40"

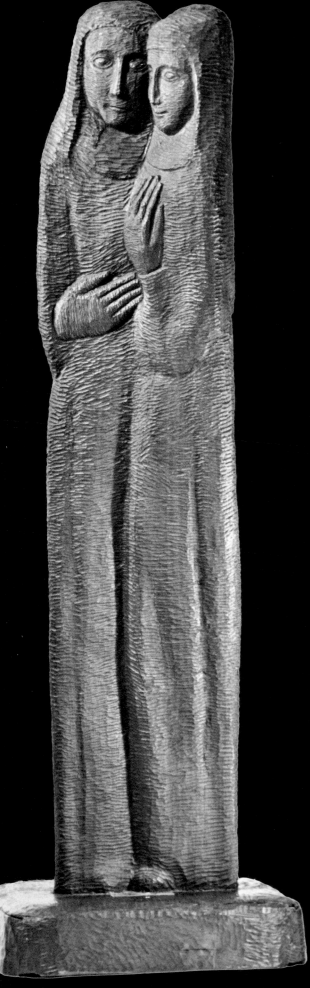

DETAIL

RUTH AND NAOMI
Walnut
66"

25

MOTHER SETON
Stoneware
27½"

ST. FRANCIS
Walnut
32"

**QUEEN OF THE UNIVERSE**
Pittsford marble
72"

FLIGHT INTO EGYPT
Walnut
48"

"COULD YOU NOT WATCH
ONE HOUR  WITH ME"
Walnut pulpit
46"

GOOD SHEPHERD (detail)
Walnut
96"

CRUCIFIXION AND RESURRECTION
Welded steel with crystal
21"

CRUCIFIX
Welded steel
36"

PROCESSIONAL
CROSS (detail)
Welded steel
84"

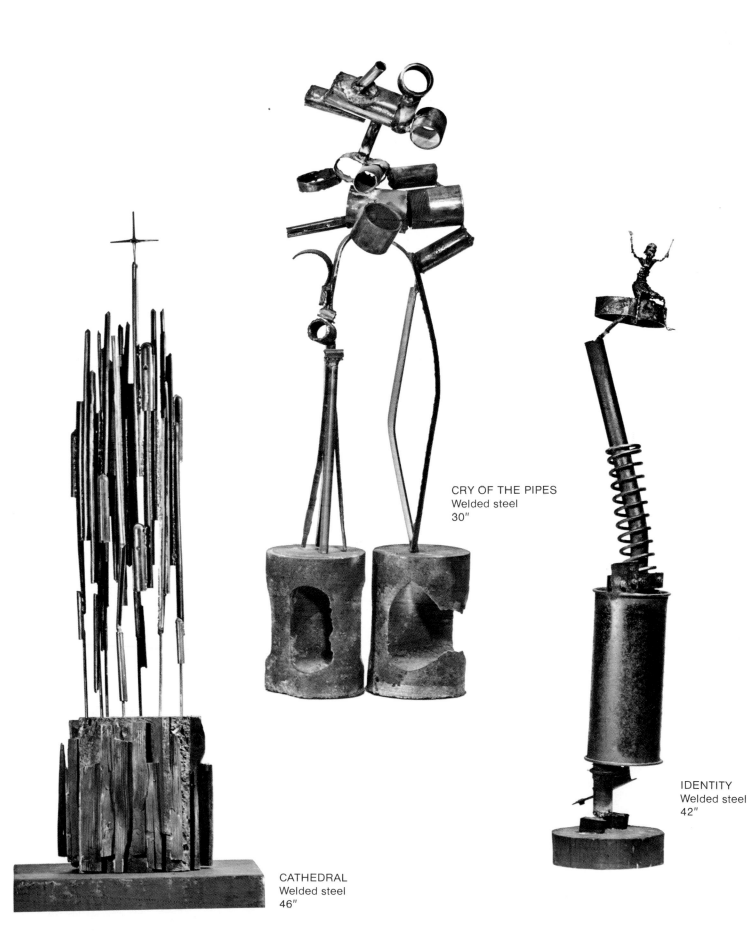

CRY OF THE PIPES
Welded steel
30″

CATHEDRAL
Welded steel
46″

IDENTITY
Welded steel
42″

31

RESURRECTION
Aluminum
53″

MARY QUEEN MOTHER
Aluminum
96″

OUR KING IS COMING
Stitching and applique
59" x 58"

DETAIL

CREATION
Hooking
65" x 42"

SHALOM
Stitching
56" x 40"

33

JOSEPH'S TECHNICOLORED COAT
Stitching and applique
Five panels, each 78" x 30"

DETAIL

34

CHRIST BLESSING THE CHILDREN
Oil
24" x 36"

WISEMEN
Oil
28" x 34"

"TAKE AND EAT, THIS IS MY BODY"
Oil
33" x 24"

"I WILL RAISE HIM UP"
Stitching
62" x 27½"

THE ETERNAL WOMAN
Walnut, with stitched cape
60"

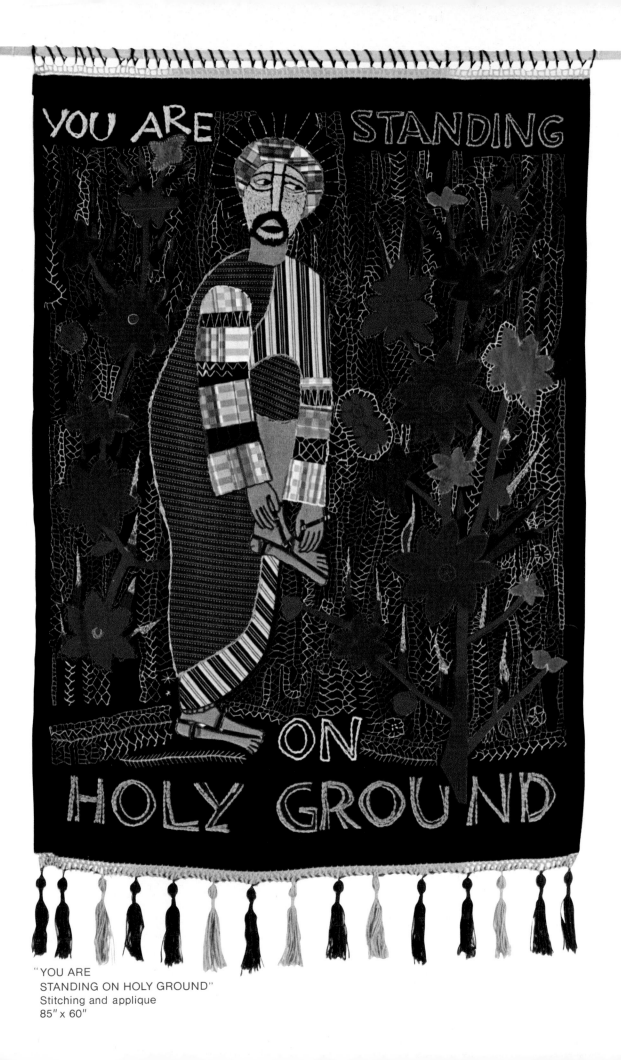

"YOU ARE
STANDING ON HOLY GROUND"
Stitching and applique
85" x 60"

VESTMENTS
Stitching and applique

CANTICLE OF THE SUN
Stitching and applique
76" x 42"

MAKE A JOYFUL NOISE
Stoneware and walnut
35″

SEAT OF WISDOM
Walnut
20″

PIETA
Blue Connecticut marble
36"

ADAM AND EVE
Cast aluminum
18"

WARSAW GHETTO
Cast aluminum
12½"

"WORTHY IS THE LAMB"
Mosaic
24" x 31"

PRODIGAL SON
Stoneware
16″

ST. FRANCIS
Aluminum
56"

"BEHOLD, I MAKE ALL THINGS NEW"
Mosaic
66" x 72"

FAMILY
Stoneware
27"

MARY, WOMAN OF GRACE
Lindenwood
48"

46

GROUP WITH CHRIST, ST. PAUL,
ST. BENEDICT
Mahogany
54″

ST. FRANCIS RECEIVING THE STIGMATA
Pencil
20½″ x 42″

JONAS IN THE WHALE (1st day)
Elm and gypsum
43"

JONAS IN THE WHALE (3rd day)
Elm and gypsum
58"

EASTER MORN
Cement relief
29" x 25½"

MOTHER OF FAIR LOVE
Ash
48"

FORGIVENESS AND
REPENTANCE
Marble relief
55" x 12"

51

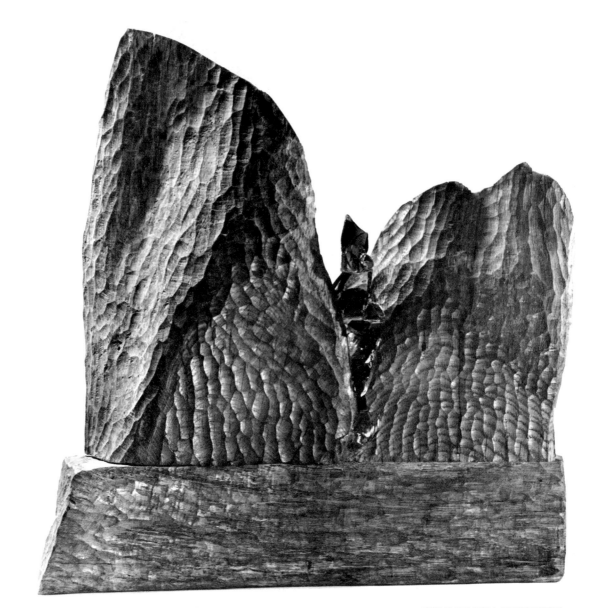

COMMUNION IN TRINITY
Cherry and faceted glass
22"

VISITATION
Plaster
60″

MAKE STRAIGHT THE WAY
Walnut
34"

JESUS CHRIST SUPERSTAR
Walnut
96"

TWO IN ONE FLESH
Walnut
74"

FATHERHOOD
Limestone
16½"

THE LISTENER
Walnut
13"

FATHER, SON,
AND SISTER SPIRIT
Walnut
15"

MARY IN CONTEMPLATION
Walnut
48"

MEN IN THE FIERY FURNACE
Walnut
26"

"COME UNTO ME"
Mahogany
92"

**JESUS CHRIST VICTOR**
Cement and walnut
84"

# Sister Helena Steffens-meier

## ACTIVITIES

Past activities include: Chairman, Alverno College Art Department, 10 years; Board Member, Wisconsin Art Educational Association; Area Chairman, Protovin, Dubuque Diocesan Art Workshops; Art Consultant, Alverno Campus Elementary School; Lecturer to Parent and Teacher Associations and to Parish Groups; Conductor of Art Workshops for Teachers; Art Seminar Professor, Catholic University; Exhibition Chairman and Regional Director, Catholic Art Association; Art Consultant, Religion Series, **A Time for Living;** Art Workshop Leader for Secondary Teachers in San Jose, Costa Rica.

## MEMBERSHIPS

Wisconsin Painters and Sculptors, Wisconsin Designers Craftsmen, National Art Education Association, American Society for Church Architecture, Catholic Art Association, Milwaukee Art Center, College Art Association; honorary member, Catholic Fine Arts Society

## PUBLICATIONS

**Art Syllabus and Manual for the Elementary Schools,** published by Silver, Burdett and Co., 1961

Art works included in books: **Applique Old and New,** by Nedda Anders, 1968; **Banners,** by Andersen and Caemmerer, 1968; **Making Contemporary Rugs and Wallhangings,** by Dona Meilach, 1970; **Textile Art in the Church,** by Marion P. Ireland, 1971; **Designing in Stitching and Applique,** by Nancy Belfer, 1972; **Creating in Cloth,** by Judith Schoener Kalina, 1976

## EXHIBITIONS

Invitational exhibits include galleries in the West: California and Washington; in the Midwest: Kansas, Illinois, Michigan, Wisconsin, Ohio, Missouri; in the East: Pennsylvania, New York, at the Metropolitan and Contemporary Crafts, and Old Westbury Gardens, Long Island

One-woman shows throughout the United States as well as in Canada

## AWARDS

Sculpture award, Wisconsin Painters and Sculptors Exhibition, Milwaukee Art Center, 1955

Drawing Competition Award, Cincinnati, Ohio, 1956

Painting Award, Fine Arts Society, New York, 1964

National Leby Memorial Award, Embroiderers Guild, Pittsburgh, 1965

Stitchery Award, Illinois Wesley Art Festival, Aurora, Illinois, 1966

Top Award for Stitching in Wisconsin Designers Craftsmen Exhibit, Milwaukee Art Center, 1967

Top Award for Stitchery in Liturgical Arts Division of Exhibition '70, Columbus, Ohio

Top Award for Sculpture, Mayfair Exhibition, Milwaukee, 1976

Medal Award and Honorary Membership for Artistic Achievements in the Fine Arts Society, Maryland, 1967

Citation in Acknowledgement of Distinctive Work, Alverno College, Milwaukee, 1968

Listing in **Notable Americans of 1976-77** and receiving of Notable Americans Award

Inclusion in 1977, Vol. XIV, **Dictionary of International Biography**

Inclusion in 1977, Fourth Edition of **The World Who's Who of Women**

## TRAVEL

Greece, Syria, Lebanon, Israel, Jordan, Mexico, Spain, France, Italy, England, Germany, Costa Rica, and Guatemala

# Chronology of Sister Helena Steffens-meier's major art works

## The following listing represents other major pieces not included in this book.

BLESSED MOTHER, Walnut, 26", 1958, *Saint Henry Church, Owassa, OK*
CHALICE, Silver, 1958, *Rev. Carroll, Chicago, IL*
HEAD OF CHRIST, Vermont marble, 15", 1958, *Mrs. Chen, Milwaukee, WI*
SAINT HENRY, Walnut, 28", 1958, *Saint Henry Church, Owassa, OK*
SAINT JOSEPH, Walnut, 27", 1958, *Saint Henry Church, Owassa, OK*
MOTHER IN THE MACABLES, Mahogany, 84", 1960, *Dr. Ruggero, Wonderlake, WI*
CIBORIUM, Silver set with diamond, 1961, *St. James Church, St. Paul, IA*
SIMEON STYLYTE, 84" x 16" x 16", Plaster model for bronze casting, 1961
THE PLEROMA, Oil, 30" x 36", 1962
HEAVENLY JERUSALEM, Oil, 40" x 30", 1963, *Dr. & Mrs. Craig Larson, Milwaukee, WI*
THE MUSTARD SEED, Oil, 20½" x 40", 1963
HEAD OF CHRIST, Walnut, 14", 1964, *Mr. John Poncha, Vice President and Prime Minister of West Cameroon, Africa*
THE FOUR HORSEMEN, Oil, 31½" x 42", 1965
IMPOVERISHED, Oil, 30" x 38", 1965
PALM SUNDAY, Stitching and applique, 54" x 23½", 1965, *St. James Anglican Church, Dundas, Ontario*
SAINT CLARE, Walnut, 54", 1965, *Mary of the Angels Convent, Omaha, NE*
ESTHER, Alabaster, 10" x 8" x 8½", 1966
HIS NAME SHALL BE CALLED EMMANUEL, Stitching, 48" x 96", 1966, *St. Thomas Anglican Church, Toronto, Ontario*
SAINT FRANCIS, Aluminum leaf over molded polystyrene, 48", 1966, *Dr. & Mrs. Craig Larson, Milwaukee, WI*
ST. FRANCIS IN ECSTASY, Ceramic, 20" x 11" x 5", 1966
SUFFERING CHRIST WITH CHILDREN, Woodcut, 20" x 25", 1966
"UNTO YOU, O LORD", Hooking, 29" x 37", 1966
GOOD SHEPHERD, Walnut, 30" x 10" x 7½", 1967
"HE COMETH WITH THE CLOUDS", Batik, 39" x 30½", 1967
MARANATHA, Oil, 31" x 41", 1967
MOTHER LOVE, Walnut, 49" x 10" x 3½", 1967
"THIS IS MY BODY", Walnut, 20" x 30" x 12", 1967, *Rev. Grendler, Sutherland, IA*
"YAHWEH IS KING", Stitching, 53" x 34", 1967
DESIGN FOR 14 WINDOWS AND FRONT DOORS, Wrought iron and glass, 1969, *Cathedral Tileran, Costa Rica, Central America*
EVERYBODY'S WORLD, Oil, 54" x 25½", 1969
RESURRECTION, Stitching and applique, 47½" x 98", 1969
DO THIS IN REMEMBRANCE OF ME, Oak relief, 18½" x 67½", 1970
THE ELEMENTS, Stitching, 102" x 29", 1970
"GATES, RAISE YOUR ARCHES", Stitching and applique, 97" x 30", 1970
SARA, Batik on paper, 30" x 19½", 1970
SEEKING-FINDING, Stitching, 68" x 22", 1970
THE MARKET IN GUATEMALA, Oil, 48" x 96", 1970, *Alverno College Library*
THE PLEROMA, Oil, 54" x 25½", 1970, *Rev. Bernard Pertzborn, Madison, WI*
THE SPIRIT IS A-MOVIN', Crayon and acrylic, 31" x 25", 1970
MIRACULOUS DRAUGHT OF FISHES, Stitching and applique, 50" x 67", 1972
PENTECOST, Stitching, 72" x 36", 1972
RUG, Gordion knot, 49" x 36", 1973
CHRIST'S ENTRY INTO JERUSALEM, Oil, 36" x 36", 1974, *Rev. Donald Shmauz, Madison, WI*
CROZIER, Walnut, 60", 1974, *Bishop Flores, Izabal, Guatemala, Central America*
CROZIER, Walnut, 72", 1974, *Benet Lake Abbey, IL*
CROZIER, Walnut, 72", 1974, *St. Procopius Abbey, Lille, IL*
JOSEPH IN HIS TECHNICOLORED COAT, Oil, 20" x 16", 1974, *Rev. Donald Shmauz, Madison, WI*
MAGNIFICAT, Oak relief, 64" x 14" x 4", 1974, *St. Frederick's Chapel, Cudahy, WI*
ST. FRANCIS, Walnut, 6½" x 12" x 8", *Nursing Bldg., Alverno College*
THE SPIRIT OF THE LORD REST UPON ME, Walnut, 75" x 19" x 8½", 1974
YOU CROWN THE YEAR WITH YOUR BOUNTY, Stitching and applique, 63" x 50", 1974
"YOUR GLORY FILLS THE WHOLE EARTH", Stitching and applique, 47" x 80", 1974
    *Bon Secours Hospital, Grosse Point, MI*
CRIB SET, Eight Figures, Stoneware, 27", 1975, *Sisters of St. Joseph of the Third Order of St. Francis, Bartlett, IL*
"I AM THE CHRIST", Stitching and applique, 73" x 19", 1976
MEDITATION, Walnut, 33" x 10" x 10", 1976, *Mr. Jeffrey Dunn, Racine, WI*
THE TRINITY, Walnut, 12½" x 13" x 7", 1976, *Rev. Robert Ries, St. Mary Hill Hospital, Milwaukee, WI*
THE VISIT, Stitching and applique, 82" x 39", 1976, *Mr. Frank Alexander, Lake Geneva, WI*
CHRIST COMING IN GLORY, Oil, 49" x 73", 1976
JEWISH PSALMODY, Stitching and applique, 81" x 38", 1977